M000042225

How to
SURVIVE
Your Child's
MISSION

How to
SURVIVE
Your Child's
MISSION

Gail Jennings Tietjen

CFI
Springville, Utah

© 2009 Gail Jennings Tietjen

All rights reserved.

No part of this book may be reproduced in any form whatsoever, whether by graphic, visual, electronic, film, microfilm, tape recording, or any other means, without prior written permission of the publisher, except in the case of brief passages embodied in critical reviews and articles.

This is not an official publication of The Church of Jesus Christ of Latter-day Saints. The opinions and views expressed herein belong solely to the author and do not necessarily represent the opinions or views of Cedar Fort, Inc. Permission for the use of sources, graphics, and photos is also solely the responsibility of the author.

ISBN 13: 978-1-59955-295-8

Published by CFI, an imprint of Cedar Fort, Inc., 2373 W. 700 S., Springville, UT 84663
Distributed by Cedar Fort, Inc., www.cedarfort.com

LIBRARY OF CONGRESS CATALOGING-IN-PUBLICATION DATA

Tietjen, Gail Jennings, 1945-
  How to survive your child's mission : a parent's perspective / Gail Jennings Tietjen.
    p. cm.
  ISBN 978-1-59955-295-8
  1. Mormon missionaries. 2. Parent and child--Religious aspects--Church of
Jesus Christ of Latter-day Saints. 3. Church of Jesus Christ of Latter-day
Saints--Missions. 4. Mormon Church--Missions. I. Title.

  BX8661.T54 2009
  266'.930835--dc22

    2009032029

Illustrations by Gail Jennings-Tietjen
Cover design by Jen Boss
Cover design © 2009 by Lyle Mortimer
Edited and typeset by Heidi Doxey

Printed in the United States of America

10 9 8 7 6 5 4 3 2 1

Printed on acid-free paper

For my sons, Darren, Roosevelt, Donnie, and
Jamie and my husband, Mel.

And dedicated to missionary parents the world
over who sacrifice precious years with their
children to ensure the Gospel of Jesus Christ is
brought to all the nations of the earth.
Thank you.

CONTENTS

FOREWORD

Are the characteristics of nurturing and worrying both found within your definition of a good parent? If your answer is yes, then you'll be able to relate to the concepts and emotions illustrated within this book as you send your child into the mission field.

Often we spend years preparing our children to serve the Lord, not realizing we, ourselves, may need some preparation to manage the emotions we feel sending our beloved child into the unknown. I hope that reading this book will not only relieve any sense that you might be alone in your feelings of anxiousness and concern, but it will also provide helpful suggestions focused at surviving such emotions.

With both her wit and hard-earned wisdom, Gail does an exceptional job of guiding the novice parent through the experience of being "the parent left behind."

Kevin Theriot, PhD

Kevin Theriot, PhD, received his doctorate from Arizona State University and is not only a private practitioner, but has been a dedicated staff therapist for The Church of Jesus Christ of Latter-day Saints Social Services for the past thirty years.

I Hope They Call Him on a Mission

TRUE **Confessions**

This is the day you've been waiting for. Your child has chosen to spend the next two years of his life in full-time service to the Lord. You're thrilled! You're excited! You're crying your eyes out because he's leaving home! Guess what . . . you're not alone.

Dickens' famous words, "It was the best of times, it was the worst of times" suddenly became the only words that could describe my feelings! I sat in the temple, attempting to choke back the tears. I blotted my eyes and hoped I was being discreet, lest those more stalwart women seated around me should notice that I was in danger of being reduced to a blithering mass of motherly wreckage! I felt so inferior to the other mothers in the session who seemed so composed.

Why was I like this? Wasn't this the day I had been waiting for? All around me were smiling faces. Sweet sisters dressed in white would glance at the tag adorning my shoulder that proclaimed me to be a "Missionary Mother."

"Where is your son going?" they'd ask with little regard as to how many times I must have answered that question.

"Michigan," I replied, trying to supply them with the excitement and the commitment I knew I should emote.

"Isn't that wonderful?" would be the reply. "You must be thrilled!"

"Oh, yes, I couldn't be happier," came my dutiful response.

"Is this your first son to go?" The phrase sounded so appropriate.

"Actually, no, my oldest son is serving in Hawaii, and I have another who just arrived in the New Jersey Mission a week ago."

"Three at once . . . isn't that amazing?" My mind immediately turned to the phrase "three in one blow" from the children's fairy tale where the little tailor swatted three flies with one swing. I had to dismiss that thought; it did nothing to cheer me up!

The fact that there was yet another son left at home seemed little consolation. I thought this was surely how Abraham must have felt when he was asked to sacrifice Isaac. If only it was that way for me. You know, the Lord would say, "Daughter, your willingness to sacrifice is enough. Your sons don't have to go." Alas, I knew this would not be the case. *What a crazy thought!* Didn't I want them to go? Didn't I want them to serve the Lord? Didn't I know this was an opportunity unlike any other to learn the gospel? Didn't I remember the blessings promised to those who would bring but one soul unto the Lord?

Of course I did! I wanted them to go—I just wanted to go along with them. Or, if that idea was unacceptable, why couldn't they serve and still live at home?

Again, I remembered where I was and made a noble effort at composure. My husband glanced at me from where he was seated. He smiled, giving me that all-knowing look as if to say, *Isn't this great, honey? This is what we've looked forward to all these years.* I hoped my own smile was a confirmation of his thoughts. I say "hoped" because my mind was thinking, *Oh sure, easy for you to say. You have your business and duties as a bishop to take your mind off things. No wonder you're not as miserable as I am.* Men! What did they know, anyway? We're always hearing talks about how much more compassionate and caring women are. Obviously, that was the difference!

There were two other "Missionary Mothers" going through the same session I was. I saw this as my chance to commiserate, a chance to see that others had the same less-than-noble feelings as I, a chance to vindicate myself of my imperfection. I glanced down the row trying to make eye contact with the one sitting a few seats down from me. I knew I would find a tear-stained cheek to add credence to my own feelings of woe. What was this? A happy relaxed countenance? Obviously an imposter, probably not a mother at all, but merely a close friend standing in, a proxy. I had heard of that before.

I turned to the "Missionary Mom" seated next to me. A wave of shock went through me when I saw her head bobbing as she strained to stay awake. I recalled our conversation in which she told me she had eight children in all, and this son was the oldest. Well, she's probably relieved to get rid of one, I thought. Then my eyes drifted to my son sitting next to his dad, beaming with excitement, pride, and anticipation. The glorious power of the Spirit pushed the rebellion far into the recesses of my soul, and I was able to enjoy the wonder of the session.

I thought that nothing could compare with that feeling of having your children there with you in the temple.

The feelings that I am confessing now were something that I felt guilty to express at the time. I thought I was the only one who felt that way and that people would think less of me if I expressed them. Only the closest of friends were allowed to enter into this gloomy portion of my mind. Now, however, I can make these confessions, knowing that I am not so unusual, I am not less spiritual than anyone else—I am just a mom! So, on with the confessions.

When my second son left, I was definitely a basket case. All of my senses seemed to work against me—sight, for example. Upon taking him to the airport and returning home, I cried when I saw his car parked in the driveway (something I had also done when his older brother left). I cried when I walked past the door to his room and visualized him perched on his bed, strumming his guitar.

Then there was sound. He was musically talented, and I chose to torture myself by listening to tapes of him singing as I blubbered along in choked-up harmony. Touch was difficult. I tried hugging his clothes and stroking his face in his pictures as if they had dimension. Holding his favorite possessions also seemed to help make me miserable, a condition I seemed to be striving for.

Smell! I really knew I was losing it when I found one of his shirts that hadn't as yet gone through the wash. I was like a starving dog who had found a tidbit of steak under the dining table. I grasped the shirt in both hands, smothering my face into it. I could still smell the scent of his cologne. I inhaled and cried, inhaled and cried. It's a miracle that I didn't suck the buttons right off the shirt. I carried the shirt from room to room, every now and then taking time to get yet another precious whiff. Would it be possible to sniff all the scent out of the shirt? Maybe I should wrap it in plastic and save some scent for later! Reality kept rearing its ugly head, saying, *Gail, you're being ridiculous. Put the shirt in the wash and pack it away with the rest of his clothes.* No, no, this was the last remembrance I had, and I couldn't callously wash it away. Somehow, I eventually managed to let go and put the shirt in its proper place, a trunk in the garage, to await the return of its owner.

I wrote letters in advance of my son's leaving and mailed them ahead of time so that he would be sure to have a letter every day of his first week in the Missionary Training Center. I packed his suitcase with loving care and made sure he would not need a thing when he arrived at the MTC, but, just in case, I called a friend who lived in Provo and had treats delivered. I made sure that I had packed self-addressed, stamped envelopes to insure that I too would be receiving mail. I bought the little heart stickers stating, "I ♥ my missionary." Over the top, you say? I think not! Rather, very typical and very much the same behavior as all of my friends with sons leaving at the same time.

I remember that when my first son left, I was emotionally petrified. I held everything in and exhibited my feelings through over-preparation and nervous tension, which I managed to disperse throughout the whole family. That being said, we were somehow late for the airport.

As fortune would have it, things did not go smoothly. Dad drove us to the elevator in the parking lot and told us to take the luggage and head for the gate; he would catch up. That would have been a perfect plan if he had not then backed the car over our son's foot. The blessing was that his shiny new wing-tip shoes could have supported an army tank, and, anyway, the tire only caught the toe of his shoe and didn't injure his foot. Within minutes, though frazzled, we were free to race to the gate.

When we reached the gate, it was time to board the plane, and the flight attendants quickly guided my son down the ramp. There was little time for emotion. One quick hug, a "Don't forget to write every week," a lengthy wave that lasted until he was out of sight, and that was it. We were so thankful to have made it in one piece that we were actually smiling as we waved him on.

One of the other sisters in the stake was there to see her son off and took the opportunity to tell me what a "rock" I was and what a wonderful example to those weaker, more emotional mothers, like herself, who were weeping and carrying on. I put my arm around her to give comfort and to perpetuate the idea being created in her mind, but really I had no idea what she was talking about. Inside, I was nearly paralyzed!

Fortunately, she didn't see me when we pulled into the driveway and I saw my son's truck sitting there, looking pitifully lonely for its owner. That was all it took for me to release those tears and go through the emotion that had been robbed from me at the airport.

We are all mortal beings with mortal emotions, worries, and shortcomings. As we look around at others in our neighborhoods and Church congregations, we see people with their Sunday persona, putting their best spiritual feet forward. Often, we are not allowed into the inner sanctum of their personal thoughts, but nevertheless, they have them, and these people are, more than likely, much like all the rest of us.

I remember working in the kitchen after a ward dinner and enjoying chatting with some of the other women. There was a situation with one of my sons that I was concerned about but had never shared with anyone because I thought they would think ill of him and know that my family wasn't perfect like I imagined theirs to be.

It wasn't long until one of the moms confided that she was worried about her daughter who, though she had been active all of her life, had just married out of the Church. Another spoke of her child who had decided not to go to Church, a third thought she would never see her son graduate from high school and another had the difficult task of seeing her child through a life-threatening illness.

They all had faith in the Lord, but this didn't keep them from worrying and going through difficult times in their roles as mothers. I hate to admit that, though my heart ached for their individual problems, I sensed an inner feeling of relief that we were all the same. Each of us had challenges in life and had to rise to meet them as best we could with the help of Heavenly Father.

From that day forth, I handled my problems better, knowing there were situations I wasn't aware of among the members in my ward family. Again, I realized that problems and challenges were not mine alone to bear. We were all on this earth for the same reason, and though each would have different challenges, we would all have them.

This same principle holds true with regard to our reactions when our offspring leave the nest to serve the Lord. The dominant thought is how grateful we are that they are spiritually worthy and physically and mentally prepared. We savor the thought that there may be specific folks out there to whom they are being sent, to teach and to change lives in the eternal sense. Secondary to that, we are excited at the prospect of what this mission will give back in the way of blessings, education, and general attitude. Third, though we are happy that we have a child giving this service to the Lord, we will miss him, because we love him.

To each parent who is dealing with the emotion of separating from a missionary son or daughter, I would like to say: You are not so unusual. You are a good person, a good mother or father, and the fact that your inner thoughts are somewhat less than noble—or not, at least, what you have always considered to be noble—they will not keep you out of the celestial kingdom. When I define noble thoughts, I think of loving our children enough to worry and being faithful enough to send them off with joy in your heart and a lump in your throat.

Choosing to prepare your son for a mission was your calling, and you did it well! Now you must send him off, and if you shed a tear in the process . . . know that it's okay.

Your **Feelings** of **Loss** Are Great

You've admitted it to yourself. You feel a great loss. You may have even admitted it to others and realized that you are not alone. When a child leaves the home, it can bring about great emotional distress. You want to be "noble," but your heart is breaking.

It was after the farewell meeting for one of my sons that the inspiration to write this book first came to me. I was not doing well. When I had stood before the congregation at my son's farewell, I had equated the feelings of his leaving to those I would have felt if someone died! I'm sure I caused many to gasp at my lack of spiritual strength, but not so for one sister in the congregation.

After the meeting, she made her way down the aisle and took my hand in hers. "You're the first mother that I've ever heard tell the truth," she said. "The way it feels is the best-kept secret in the Church."

Hmmm, I thought. I guess I was a little unusual in

my willingness to boldly share my shortcomings or lack of "spiritual giant" status. However, as I have said, it is important to know that there are many out there who share these feelings and that you are not the only one who is sad or worried. And finally, though you think it will never pass, it does.

During the years that followed, I found myself being more keenly aware of the feelings of missionary moms as their "babies" were about to leave the nest. I have to admit that I was always surprised to find those less emotional moms who saw that this was the exact thing they had wanted for this child since birth. It was the culmination of hopes and prayers. These thoughts seemed to take away any sense of loss, loneliness, or worry.

At first, I thought that these were the women who were more perfect than me, who had always given their children freedom to make their own decisions and were never controlling. Therefore, they did not feel the need to oversee or stay in control. Their children must have been gospel scholars, obedient to the extreme, and definitely General Authority material.

Through further observation, I found that this could be the case in a few situations but, more than likely, it was a matter of personality. When the son of a stake president left, a friend called his wife the following day and asked how she was doing. Her husband replied that she was, at that very moment, curled up in the fetal position on the couch, sobbing.

This was a good woman, a great mom, and a strong sister who was active in the Church and community. This good woman was feeling loss, the loss that is, for some, akin to a death in the family. So, there must be reasons that we feel this loss, but what are they?

- A loss of identity or job description. You are no longer needed to nurture. Even if you are needed, you cannot be there physically and will have to cover it in a letter.
- A loss of control. If you are a controller, you have to quit cold turkey! He is on his own and, good or bad, his decisions are his own.
- A loss of companionship. If you are a single parent, this can be severe. If your child is a friend as well as a family member, you are losing both of these entities.
- A loss of support. You may be losing someone who is physically and emotionally helpful and comforting.
- A change in family structure. The family dynamic has changed. There is a hole that is left, like a missing piece of a puzzle, and that piece is lost until the missionary brings it back. No other piece will complete the puzzle and make the picture the same.
- A change in him. We have a fear that, though our child will return, he will be forever different. He will come back with new goals, and his place will never be the same in the family unit. Soon after his return, he will leave for college or get married. This is really the end of something. Again, this is what we want, but it is another sense of loss lurking on the horizon.
- Last, but not least, you're just being a mom!

I recently spoke with the mom of a returned missionary who went through enormous feelings of loss when her missionary left. With time and wonderful letters, these feelings subsided, and there was great joy and comfort when he returned with honor.

However, it was not long after his return that he met the young woman with whom he wanted to spend the rest of his life, and the same feelings of loss returned for his mother. This time it was different in that the worries were different: Was he ready for marriage? Would he continue his schooling?

The reality is that when the child is ready for marriage, the picture puzzle is put on the shelf and a whole new family puzzle takes its place with more pieces to include: sons-in-law, daughters-in-law, and grandchildren. Then we can start worrying and grieving all over again when our grandchildren go on missions!

So, we've said that these feelings pass. How does that happen? When does that happen? When you're going through it, it doesn't seem possible that the pain in your heart will ever go away.

Hooray for the MTC! The first ray of hope will occur after your child has been in the Missionary Training Center for about a week. The first letter is usually a good one, and by the second week, you will be amazed. When you start getting the wonderful letters from this person in the MTC—and you wonder who he is and why he is impersonating your missionary—you will not only feel better, you will feel great. The spirit is so strong there that it can be put on paper, placed in an envelope, and delivered to your home on a weekly basis.

Even for those learning difficult languages, life at the MTC seems to be a highlight of their missions, and they are armed for the two years ahead. The time spent there and the things learned fill in all the gaps that you were worried about in the training you gave at home. When they leave the MTC, these young missionaries are now soldiers in the army of God—and never doubt that He does lead His army.

You must allow yourself human frailties. Don't judge yourself harshly if tears are shed, for the Lord knows your heart. Enjoy this time. Enjoy the well-wishes of your friends. Enjoy the light that surrounds your son or daughter. This, after all, is not the ending of a novel, but the beginning of a new and exciting chapter.

Is he homesick? Do the members support him?
Is he healthy? Is he eating right? Is he praying?
Is he taking care of his clothes? Does he like his
companion? Does his companion like him?

When They **Tell** You **Not** to Worry

Your "baby" is going off to parts unknown, probably for the first time. But why should you worry? Because you're the mom, that's why! It's your job!

Don't you just hate that! After all, what has your job been for the last eighteen years? Has your worrying not gotten every meal on the table, arranged every birthday party, and prevented many winter colds by insuring each child had the proper clothing when heading out the door in the morning? Many an embarrassing cowlick has been prevented by a mom licking her fingers and wetting down the wayward hair as a child bolted out the door for an important event.

For years, you have been there to walk them to school or see that they were safely on a school bus to take them a few blocks or a few miles away, and, even then, they would only be gone a few short hours. Can you still hear your parting words, "Don't talk to strangers"?

When a young person sets out for a foreign country, or even for another state, you are supposed to put this young man or young woman on a plane, alone, knowing you won't see him or her for two years, and knowing this novice to worldly things is going half a world away. Who will physically be there to be sure she is eating properly? Who will sit by his bedside all night when he has a fever? And who will be sure that the dreaded colors don't get in with the whites in the wash, thereby leaving this servant of the Lord with pink underwear?

The truthful answer is . . . no one. Yes, the boy will have to survive on things he never dreamed of eating before. The once-frowned-upon brussel sprouts may suddenly look good to him! Your daughter will get through illnesses with the help of her companion who is, possibly, a mere six months older than she and not any wiser. And your son will learn to get the dreaded pink dye out of his own underwear.

You say that these are not the most comforting words you have ever heard? That's okay. The Lord is not going to punish you for worrying. As a matter of fact, it won't be long until he sees that you have perfected that skill, and he will give you the comfort and peace of mind that you never realized was possible. I assure you that I am as good a worrier as you are, and I too was able to attain peace in my heart.

As my family was growing up, I took pride in my ability to worry about everything and take it to a level of total self-consumption. To feel better about it, I would call it multi-tasking! When I had nothing of my own to worry about, I would worry about everyone else's problems and call it concern.

This gave me great status in life as a person of true

understanding and empathy, and one generous with her time and means. Of course, this statement is meant to be tongue in cheek, but be careful. Sometimes, we equate these qualities with who we are, and when the ability to bestow this worry, this motherly concern, on our primary target is taken away, we get confused as to what our job is and who we are. This can cause depression, and we may not recognize it for what it is.

We assume we are missing our beloved child, but really, we are floundering to readjust to our new job description. In most cases, another child or our husband is right there, happy to soak up any leftover worrying and spoiling. If you happen to be alone, your problem is greater, but with little effort you can find a myriad of good works to do, which will be the best medicine for what ails you.

So we haven't actually said that there is nothing to worry about when your child goes on a mission. Did you notice that? The Lord does not take away everyone else's agency in order to protect your child. That is not the plan. Yes, they will have companions who drive them crazy, or they may be the companion who drives everyone else crazy. They may get sick, or homesick, or get in an accident. They may suffer inconveniences or dangers that they would not be exposed to at home.

The sons of Mosiah were cast out, spat upon, and imprisoned. In worst-case scenarios, similar things can still happen today. We know what goes on in the world and we can see that bad things can happen, even when in the service of the Lord. Indeed, we may know someone who has experienced the severe tragedy of losing a child, and it is hard to imagine anything more difficult to endure. But here comes the big *however.*

However, danger exists throughout our lives, no matter where we are. We are tempted by Satan, no matter where we are. We can be hit by a car, no matter where we are. We can be the victim of illness, no matter where we are. So, what do you choose? When your child chooses to go on a mission, you must, in the deepest recesses of your motherly, bleeding heart, choose it for him also.

Our issue as mothers is that we have always felt somewhat in control of these things, if our offspring were nearby. When they were small, we could hold their hands crossing the street. As they grew older, we could remind them to buckle-up or to take a sweater when they went out. But now, oh, no! They are out of our control!

This is not a comfortable place to be. When we keep reminding ourselves that we have chosen this path for our children, chosen it because we know what a great gift this can be to others, chosen it because we know what great changes can be brought about in their lives by serving missions, chosen it because we know the gospel is true, and chosen it because we love the Lord, we can control the control issue!

I don't want to leave this topic without talking about what should be obvious. That is, the safety net that is in place for our missionaries in the field. First and foremost, this glorious Church is led by a prophet of God. He and the other General Authorities are well aware of what is going on in the world and are constantly concerned with how this will affect our missionaries. They have a finger on the pulse of this program and can make decisions, at any moment, to change or institute a policy to benefit and protect our sons and daughters. The Church has a marvelous network that can disseminate information to all parts of the world in a very short period of time.

We know that choice men have given of their time to serve as mission presidents all over the world. They make themselves familiar with the culture and laws of the land where they serve, and they can guide our missionaries to prevent many problems that could occur due to sheer ignorance of customs. Moreover, the mantle placed on them provides specific inspiration and abilities that are God-given.

The Lord also blesses and assists mission presidents in shepherding their flocks. They have direct knowledge of each of their missionaries through zone leaders and below them, district leaders, and, of course, companions. The mission president will know if your child is ill and will help to make decisions regarding appropriate care. If anything at all serious is going on, you will be notified, and if continued treatment is necessary, your missionary may even be returned home temporarily for treatment.

An important person, who is always hovering in the background as the unsung heroine, is the mission president's wife. She is the mission mom and, though she is not always in the forefront, I have never spoken with a missionary who had not been blessed in some way by this partner in service. It is wonderful to know that there is a person with the same motherly concern that we have, watching over these young servants of the Lord.

Perhaps the greatest comfort to me, while my boys were serving, was the knowledge that each of them seemed to have members that they became close to, who took them in, fed them a meal, and gave them a taste of home away from home. I hoped those members would also assist in helping my boys to avoid any huge pitfalls.

I knew that this was an additional network of people that I could count on to be aware if anything seemed unusual. To these wonderful saints in Hawaii, Michigan, and New Jersey, I will always be grateful.

Last, but surely not least, we must remember that possibly never in their lives have more prayers been offered for the success and well-being of these young people. Saints all over the world, in every language and tongue, are praying daily for the success and well-being of the missionaries. Each one does not need to be mentioned by name, for their Heavenly Father knows each one individually. He knows who they are, where they are, and what they need.

We must arm our missionaries with the greatest tool, the most powerful weapon they can take with them—the willingness to humble themselves in prayer. If they are not used to it at home, they will not suddenly develop this trait in the mission field. You may not be there, mom or dad, to hand your boy his sweater when he goes out the door, but if you have taught him to pray—to pray always, to pray diligently—he will walk hand in hand with his ultimate parent, his Heavenly Father.

Cupid's song can be lethal to those who desire to serve a mission.

Watch Out for Cupid

—Those Arrows Can

Be Lethal

Any degree of romantic involvement is something to contend with, especially for those planning to serve a mission. Following the admonitions of the prophet will keep our children untarnished and worthy.

Now that we've decided we are happy and rejoicing at the thought that we have a child who is desirous to serve a mission, we have a parental responsibility to provide guidance in helping that child remain ready and worthy to serve. As you may know, the bar has been raised, and the leaders of our Church want to be sure our young people are as physically and spiritually prepared as possible to take on this great task before them.

We have the duty to lead and guide as best we can to help our youth over the hurdles that might prevent them from accepting this calling. One of the biggest hurdles to overcome may be the one placed there by that sly little arrow-toting fellow in diapers that we know as Cupid!

Our youth may decide that they are "in love" one or more times during their teenage years. We should keep in mind that this probably won't happen if they are not dating! It would also be difficult for it to happen if relationships with the opposite sex are kept within the guidelines of the Church.

Times are not what they used to be, and, along with our children, we can allow our value system to be permeated with the ideas and ideals of the world. For some reason, parents may fear reprisal from their children when they insist that those children abide by the rules that a prophet of the Lord has given. We must ask ourselves two things:

1. Do we have a deep and abiding faith that the dating guidelines set forth within the Church program are inspired and should be followed with the same conviction as any other commandment?

2. Do we truly believe that we are showing love and concern by allowing our youth to participate in activities that put them in situations where Satan can use their natural teenage desires to bring them to destruction? Do we really believe that, when they become adults, our children will say, "Gee, thanks, Mom and Dad, for letting me stay out until all hours of the night. Thanks for letting me park in front of the house with my date instead of coming in when we got home. Thanks for letting me date at fourteen because all of my friends were doing it. Thanks for letting me wear clothing that exposed too much of my body so that I could be popular."

Somehow, I don't think that any of the above will

happen. Actually, I have heard many young girls bemoaning the fact that they did not enjoy being little girls and tried to grow up too fast. Many a tear has been shed for the young boy or girl who is suddenly thrust into the role of parenthood because they couldn't control their passions in a compromising situation.

Recently, I had the opportunity to speak with a young woman who was a freshman at a local university. She confided that she was feeling very much like an old maid because, at the ripe old age of eighteen, she hadn't yet experienced a "real kiss." I looked at this beautiful girl and, I have to confess, this surprised me as well. She was beautiful, had a great figure, was attending college on one of several scholarships offered, and had always been active in Church. So why no kiss?

In delving into the background of this situation, I realized that she had, indeed, been very popular. The blessing in her life was that her peers were also very active in the Church. They all had the same value system and goals, and supported each other in reaching these goals. Though each member of the group achieved individual popularity, they did things as a group of friends.

As in the case of this young woman, they all had dates for the proms, went on all the school trips and Church activities, participated in sports, attended seminary, and many excelled scholastically. Each had a very full and exciting youth and never felt left out of anything. This not only gives validity to the old saying, "there is safety in numbers," but it shows that group dating provides social activity and support for all, and not just the chosen few.

Suddenly, I realized that this beautiful girl of eighteen was the ideal. She was the product of the Lord's plan for our youth. She was "of good report and praiseworthy"

(Articles of Faith 1:13). She would never have to worry about a sullied reputation. She had been, and was continuing to be, prepared to be a great leader among her peers, a treasured companion to a worthy priesthood holder, and a mother who could be held up to her children as a beacon to guide them throughout the trials of their lives. She would have only the best of memories of those eighteen years of her life. This is truly what all parents should want for their young men and women.

Now, it is entirely possible that the girl with whom your son will ultimately marry and live happily ever after, or the boy who sweeps your daughter off her feet, will be someone he or she meets in high school, but even if this is true, *any* degree of romantic involvement is something to contend with for someone desiring to serve a mission. Even if a young couple is stalwart and strong enough to remain pure through a serious relationship, they may see marriage as an alternative to one or both of them serving a mission.

It would seem ideal for your son to have lots of girls who are friends, rather than lots of girlfriends. Likewise, your daughter can attend lots of activities with young men, have dates for proms, and become adept at socializing with the opposite sex without going steady until after a young man's mission. We would not wish anyone to be a social outcast or miss out on the wonderful activities of youth, but the pressures of individual couple dating can make it difficult to maintain a status of untarnished morality.

Some parents find it hard to deal with telling their son that a sweet and precious girl he has known for years could be a problem for him, so instead they rationalize that nothing could ever go wrong between two such great kids from such wonderful homes. So many times, I have heard the phrase, "But his (or her) father is a bishop!" If you think there is any possibility that you are one of these parents, it's time for a reality check!

If you have any control over your teenagers, do what you can to insure that they are not burdened by a relationship that makes the decision to go on a mission more difficult. The Church's dating standards for our children may seem archaic to the outside world, but they are set forth by a loving Father in Heaven and are a blessing to our children. I believe that, though it has not always been followed, limiting a young man to group dating until he is home from his mission has always been a standard in the Church.

What could be more sad than a boy who has prepared for his mission and saved his money but who returns from his bishop's interview only to tell his parents that he is not worthy to go? Repentance for indiscretions is a blessing that will happen in time, but the standards for our youth to serve in the mission field are more stringent than ever before, and sexual promiscuity will not be overlooked.

So again we pose the question, what can be done? An obvious answer is to follow the teachings and guidelines set forth by the Church. Tough love is a lot tougher for the parents than the children, but we have to do it. Now, I realize that times are hard and that parenting isn't easy. If your children have been making decisions for themselves, and possibly for the entire family, since age five, it will be difficult to exert influence over them now. Should you throw up your hands and say, "Oh well, I can't tell him what to do"? Of course not! How many times does the Lord tell us the same things over and over again, hoping that one day we will understand and change course in our direction. If you are sincere in your desire to help your son or daughter be ready and worthy to serve a mission, the Lord is absolutely in your corner protecting and encouraging you.

Many parents have success in helping teenagers stay on the straight and narrow path by saturating them in extracurricular activities. We have to remember that children can stress out just like adults, so we have to leave lots of "rest from stress" time. Boys, more so than girls, will give up time spent on activities with the opposite sex in order to have more time for participating in or watching sports, playing in a band, singing in a chorus, taking lessons of some kind, having a part-time job, going fishing, hanging out with the guys, or doing some fun activity with Dad.

The important thing is that you, as parents, make these activities available. Your home should be the one where the gang can hang out. Your cookie jar should be the one that's always full. And even if you're not the "coolest" parents in the neighborhood, try not to be the weirdest!

If there was ever a time that you entertained the thought that agency should be something that is bestowed after your children have returned from their missions, you're probably not alone! However, that is not the plan. They are ultimately the creators of their own destinies. Our job is to be the best parents that we can, using those skills and that knowledge which the gospel provides.

We love, we teach, we support, and we have faith.

The "Other Woman!"

THE **Other** WOMAN

So there's little time left before the mission and there's a special friend in the picture. What does this mean for you, your prospective missionary, and the rest of the family?

It is less likely that a young woman will leave a serious love interest behind, as she must wait an additional two years, until the age of twenty-one, to be able to serve a mission. By that time, many young women have already found their own returned missionary with whom to spend eternity and are already making plans in that direction. Therefore, I will approach the next subject from the male perspective. That being said, the same information could apply for either a young man or woman.

In the event that your son is worthy to serve a mission, but there is a girl in the picture, his leaving will be an emotional time for both of them. Hopefully, she is a member of the Church and encouraging him in his decision to serve the Lord. If so, the standards she has set for herself will support not only her personal goals, but will help him with his as well.

Even if this is the case, this is a very dangerous time, and keeping your missionary as occupied as possible with those uplifting activities we have already mentioned is imperative.

The last two weeks before your son leaves are precious to everyone. Family, friends, and girlfriend will all want to spend as much time with him as possible. During this time, an otherwise wonderful young woman can soon become someone who is vying for the time and attention of your son during those last precious moments. She may have parents at home who are advising her to be considerate of your time as a family, but this may not be the case.

Beware! Mothers, you do not want to make this sweet young woman your adversary. I have news for you . . . she will win! You will soon become very aware that she has a power over your son that you can only hope to have and an influence that you have been working for since first he exited the womb! Be aware of her feelings and try to remember, way back when, the feelings you may have had for a special young man. This girl could be the woman your son will marry and the mother of your grandchildren.

You can tell yourself that you are the adult and, of course, you will be able to deal with this situation, and you may well be. However, I would suggest that this might take some planning. You may want to sit down as a family and plan the last couple of weeks before your son leaves. This will let your son know where he is expected to be and when, without it being dictated at the time and without interfering with plans he has already made. This will also remind you that it is improbable that your son will be with you every minute, telling you how much he loves you and appreciates everything you've done for him, and clinging to each pearl of wisdom that you desire to cram into the last two weeks before he leaves.

Some have found it a good idea, and pleasant for all, to include their sons' girlfriends as well as any good guy pals in family activities such as dinners, movies, and outings. A wonderful idea is to have a family home evening, with the girlfriend present, at which you go over the rules your missionary will be expected to follow while in the field. This is an opportunity for all to commit to obeying the mission rules, especially those regarding phone calls.

The importance of positive attitudes should also be stressed. If everyone realizes how important newsy letters of encouragement are, rather than tales of personal woes, it will do much to uplift your missionary's spirit. Young ladies can be prone to writing the typical "mushy stuff" about how lonely they are or, maybe worse, how much fun they're having going out with friends. The last thing the mission president, or your son's companion, needs is a love-struck, melancholy young man to deal with. If all he can think about is what his girl may be doing or feeling back home, he is wasting a lot of his time as well as the Lord's. These issues can be dealt with before your son leaves and can be addressed in an offhand manner that should not be offensive but matter-of-fact.

Whatever your situation, whatever your feelings, this is a good time to deal with them. It is much easier to have an understanding before problems arise than to try to fix things later and risk hurt feelings. As always, seek the counsel of the Lord and know that no detail is too small or situation too inconsequential to make it a matter of prayer.

Cramming IN MEANINGFUL Experiences

If you haven't done it in eighteen years, it will be difficult to fit it into last-minute plans.

You want your young man to have wonderful memories to take with him on his mission . . . family vacations, fun home evenings, intimate talks with Mom and Dad. You've also had the thought cross your mind that when he returns from his mission, things won't be the same. He will be off to college, possibly getting married, and the dynamics of your family unit will be forever changed.

The problem is that, if you haven't fit certain things into the last eighteen years, it is probably too late to do everything you would like. Depending on when you start, however, there are things you can do, and some you will definitely want to do, that will provide loving memories.

If your children are still young, and you have many years ahead of you to create family traditions and memories, be sure and do it as soon as possible. Even small children start remembering and looking forward to familiar events. It could be how you celebrate birthdays— possibly the "birthday person" gets to choose whatever he wants for dinner, or perhaps it is always celebrated at the same place.

Your traditions may focus around holidays and vacations or daily events such as family mealtime and home evenings. Things that seem routine at the time are traditions in the making: singing, a family band, playing board games, service projects, and the like.

In my own family, when the children were small, we always had dinner by candlelight on home evening night. The dinner might consist of something as simple as mac and cheese or sandwiches, but if there was candlelight, everything seemed special. Eyes glittered in the glow and our voices were low and our spirits high as we enjoyed sharing stories and the events of the day. The boys took turns blowing out the candles, which was a big deal in those days, and our youngest dubbed the event our "candlenight dinner."

During the growing up years, we couldn't afford expensive vacations or world travel. We did, however, enjoy visiting popular amusement parks, aquariums, beaches, and campgrounds. Our oldest son had always dreamed of going to Hawaii, but our budget wouldn't permit it. In some fit of madness, I promised him that before he went on his mission, we would accompany him and a friend on a once-in-a-lifetime trip to Hawaii.

The time was drawing close, and our son's mission call was expected any day. In those days, there was quite a waiting period between the call and the departure date, and we chose not to make vacation reservations until we had the call in hand.

The big day arrived. The envelope was in his clutches, and the family was gathered around in anticipation. There it was, a call from a prophet of the Lord, Spencer W. Kimball, to serve for a period of twenty-four months . . . in the Hawaii Honolulu Mission! As you can probably guess, we changed our plans and had a smaller, family vacation close to home.

The following suggestions might give you food for thought:

- If you can afford some wonderful, once-in-a-lifetime trip, great! However, do this only if it is not a financial burden. It is never a good idea to overextend yourself financially, especially when you are about to send a missionary into the field. Whatever you do will be warmly remembered and appreciated.

  Remember that this may, in fact, be your last opportunity to accomplish a vacation with just your children, so try to be sure every family member can attend. Once young men return, they begin their own families and might not have the time or resources to join in on extended family plans.

- A family reunion, or even a long weekend getaway can create many wonderful memories. When my husband was in the stake presidency and I was the Relief Society president, we discovered we needed weekends away from the phone. We found it great fun to gather up the boys on a Friday and check into a hotel about twenty miles away to spend the weekend. The travel time was short, but we felt like we were in a different state. There were movie theaters, restaurants, swimming pools, parks, and even chapels for Sunday attendance, all nearby.

This would be something to consider that wouldn't be hard to do at the last minute. A weekend getaway could also take place at a campground that isn't too far away, or at whatever facilities are available in your area.

- A mini family reunion, with local relatives joining in, can take place at a park with everyone bringing food to share, playing games, and enjoying fellowship, if even for just a day.

- Recently, I have been putting scrapbooks together for each son. This reminded me of a very important aspect of anything you do as a family: Pictures! Pictures! Pictures! These will be a great tool in allowing wonderful bonding memories to come flooding back into your life and the lives of your children.

- One thing that was suggested to me, and that I regret not doing, was to have a family portrait taken just before the missionary leaves. Include as many members of the family as feasible—married children, their families, and those still at home. This doesn't have to be an expensive studio portrait. With today's technology, a friend with a good camera can take a picture that can produce a quality copy.

    Your missionary will show this picture many times while away for two years. I think it helps companions and members in the field to better appreciate who these young people are and what sacrifices are made to send them out.

- Be sure your prospective missionary participates in any available school and Church activities and programs this last year. You will be surprised at the warmth looking back on this will give him.

My oldest son still talks about being "Big Bird" in a ward roadshow, and my second son requested copies of skits and plays he had participated in as a youth to help a ward in his mission.

- If your son plays an instrument, it would not be appropriate to take it along—no matter how small—but he can take along his knowledge of music. This alone will help him in leading music and singing at events in the mission field. If the instrument is a piano or organ, more than likely, he will have opportunities to use his talent.

- Though this is an extremely busy time, go the extra mile to be sure the whole family is home at dinner time and, if possible, allow for some leisurely chat time afterward.

- Your family may be one that has been diligent and successful at having a regular time for family prayer. However, sometimes, as the children get older, family prayer only happens at mealtime. Work hard at reinstating prayer at a time when all family members can attend. This might be right after dinner or early in the morning.

  This will allow your missionary to hear prayers in his behalf that he knows will continue to be offered for the two years he is away. He will remember this and when he feels alone he will know that he can turn to his Heavenly Father and that others are continually praying for his safety and success.

- There are many items that missionaries are required to take into the mission field. Obtaining these items can be an experience to be shared and a fun time for the whole family. Shop for the books, luggage, alarm clocks, personal items, and so forth during the year, so that it is not a great expense nor a source of irritation during the last couple of weeks before your missionary leaves.

These are times usually shared as a mother-son or mother-daughter activity and can be special times, if planned for. However, if the whole family is involved in the planning, it brings them closer and provides a scenario that could become family tradition for others who will leave on missions. The nineteenth birthday usually provides the white shirts and ties needed. Most other clothes shopping is also done around this time. Remember, young people not only grow spiritually but also physically, and clothes should not be purchased too far in advance.

The important thing is to make the shopping an exciting part of preparation. Inviting your son out to a relaxed lunch with Mom at the mall is probably something you haven't done for a while. Along with shopping, this also provides time for some last-minute thoughts to be shared.

• Trips to the temple can be especially peaceful and uplifting if you are fortunate enough to have one close by. The whole family would benefit from a trip to the visitors' center in honor of the missionary. Perhaps dinner out or a picnic at a nearby park following the tour, weather permitting, would be appropriate.

If the temple is not close by, you may find some videos within easy access that would be good for the whole family. It is important for all to know the great responsibilities and blessings in store for someone going through the temple for the first time.

- If family home evenings have been a part of your family life, they have already provided blessings and memories that can't be created in any other setting.

- We have already talked about including friends, especially girlfriends, in a home evening where mission rules are talked about.

- Public libraries have an amazing amount of material on the people, culture, geography, weather, and foods of all countries. You can find pictures, videos, and music to add to the atmosphere, and most can be checked out. As part of teaching the basic skills suggested in the next chapter, you might plan a dinner cooked by the missionary with cuisine that may be used where he will be going. Younger brothers and sisters love to help with this, and it creates a last-minute bonding experience.

- If you are blessed to know stories from the lives of family members who have served as missionaries, they are a great resource to involve the whole family in the upcoming adventure. Reading from journals of missionaries among your ancestors and especially from converts in the family will place special importance on serving a mission.

Use your imagination as to what would make this a special time for your family. There are many things that would be wonderful, memory-making activities. The idea is not to attempt to make a list and then cram everything into an already full schedule. Rather, use the whole year and be aware of opportunities that arise in the regular course of everyday life.

"Sure, Sister Brown, brussel sprouts will be great!"

Things to **Teach,**
Things to **Learn**

There are certain basics that every missionary should know to help care for himself, no matter where he serves.

Don't chance being a shoulda, coulda, woulda! We've talked about our feelings of loss, worry, and separation. Planning and preparation can ease the stress, even if it is rather last-minute.

Create a checklist of things that your prospective missionary will probably need to know to get by without you for two years. You may be surprised that you can check off some of the items as already accomplished. The following is a partial list of ideas that you may add to as you see fit:

SPIRITUAL BASICS

- **How to study**—This includes using time wisely, marking scriptures, and so on. Stress that this is perhaps the greatest opportunity your missionary will have in life to study the gospel and that this opportunity is a major blessing of being a missionary.

- **The importance of prayer**—Your child has been praying since he was first old enough to utter sounds. You oversaw every word and expressed great delight in this great accomplishment. As children get older, personal prayer becomes just that—personal! Take time in family home evening or in a one-on-one personal chat to talk about the things that one can and should pray about. Emphasize leaving time to listen to the Spirit. You may have a special experience with prayer that you could share.

TEMPORAL THINGS

- **Basic first aid**—A CPR course is great, but often what is most valuable is a basic knowledge of how to clean and treat a wound, what to take for headaches, muscle aches, allergies, stomach flu, and so on.

- **Ironing a white shirt**—Teach the importance of looking professional and taking pride in appearance. It has been rumored that some elders only iron the front part of a shirt that shows under a suit. Can you believe it?

- **Hemming pants**—Often there is a good sister in the ward or branch who can help your elder with this, but this is not a difficult skill and will come in very handy!

- **Sewing on a button**—This might seem self-explanatory, but that is from a woman's point of view! Start with threading the needle and tying the knot.

- **Darning a hole**—Lots of moms can't do this, but if you can teach it, you can bet your missionary will at some time tear his pants or coat, or need to mend a hole in a sock or shirt. Sister missionaries will also need instruction with this skill as it goes beyond the basic.

- **Separating clothes for the wash**—Economy is foremost in a missionary's mind, and the more clothes he can cram in the washer or dryer, the cheaper it is . . . or is it? Let him know that keeping his colors separate will prolong the life of his clothes. P-day jeans will wear out other fabrics if washed together.

- **Pre-treating clothes before washing**—Stains in those collars and cuffs can set in if thrown in a dryer before getting them completely out.

- **Balancing a check book and using a debit card**—Missionaries tend to use their funds down to the penny. Make sure your son knows about the ramifications of misusing a bank account. In many areas, the missionaries have the responsibility of using a debit card for personal needs. A bank account for this purpose should be set up before he leaves on his mission. Though the mission president in the area in which your missionary lives will see that he has funds for "living expenses," this will not include things like cameras, film, bikes, or clothing. Living within one's means is imperative on a mission and throughout life.

- **Driving**—Most youth learn to drive at the legal age in their particular area. However, if that has not happened, it's time! Unless your missionary has a medical reason for not driving, it is advantageous to be able to do so.
- **Basic table manners**—If you are hoping that the members will invite your son to dinner, be sure he is the type of houseguest that will be appreciated. Also, make him aware that this food may be very dear to those offering it and that his appointments should be kept.

A stake president in our area had the good fortune of having the elders over for dinner. His wife had cooked a wonderful roast with all the trimmings. As the food was passed around the table, one of the elders refused everything that was offered him. In this case, though the young man had eaten red meat all of his life, he had recently decided not to in order to prepare for a marathon race that he would run when he returned home!

Even though the marathon was probably not something the elder should have been so concerned about while on his mission, if it was that important, he could have mentioned it to those who invited him to dinner when they made the appointment. Any dietary issues elders have should also be brought up well in advance of a scheduled dinner. In this case, the stake president's good wife tried to offer the elder other things to eat, and the stake president did not let the missionaries leave without instruction as to how they were to act if ever invited into another home in his stake.

If there is a health issue with a missionary that requires a special diet, members can work around it, but precious food, prepared and given so graciously by the members, should never be refused on a whim or because it is not a favorite. There are many countries in which the members have very little and great sacrifices are made to feed the missionaries. This food should be eaten with even more gratitude and concern. You should also teach your missionary to be polite and courteous, to offer to help clear the table, and so on.

More Temporal Skills

- **Cooking the basics**—There are certain foods that will be available almost anywhere. Make sure you teach general preparation of potatoes, beans, rice, vegetables, homemade soups, spaghetti, and a few basic casseroles. All missionaries arrive home with great expertise in the preparation of mac and cheese and peanut butter sandwiches, but even those staples might not be available or economical in some areas.

- **Leading music**—If your missionary plays the piano or sings, he will have opportunities in the mission field to use these talents. A basic knowledge of how to lead some of the more popular hymns will not be hard to learn and will come in handy, especially if your missionary is assigned to a small branch. He might also be called on at a baptism to select and lead a hymn.

w to get along with a "constant compan-
'"—Being with the same person twenty-four
rs a day, seven days a week, would be a great
culture shock to almost anyone, especially when
you have no choice about the person that will
now occupy the same space as you do for the next
several months. How to overlook things, show
compassion, gently lead, and choose your battles
can be good tips and something that some young
people may need to hear more than others.

- **A knowledge of the mission area**—As a
family, study the area to which your missionary
is assigned: culture, climate, geography, and so
on. This will make the experience more exciting
for everyone and promise a better start in getting
acclimated. Imagine the advantage of a missionary
who respects, loves, and understands the people
before meeting them. By the way, this advice
applies just as much to those called to serve state-
side since there are many cultural, religious, and
ethnic diversities in different parts of the country.

Preparing your missionary, as best you can, will be
such a comfort to you. The things we have mentioned
are such necessary skills that all family members should
participate in learning them, and all will definitely benefit
from them. Of course, these things cannot be done at the
airport! If basic skills have not been learned in teenage
years, this may be something that you have to fit into
your cramming time during the last month or so.

There will always be last-minute instruction. There
will always be great emotion flowing at the airport or
MTC farewell. Keeping the stress level as low as possible

will make the experience positive and exciting. Good preparation will eliminate a lot of the things you might worry about. You must understand for yourself and teach the rest of the family that this is the beginning of an exciting opportunity. Your family members' spirits should soar with gratitude for the blessings that lie in store for your missionary and those with whom he will come in contact.

Guardian of the Shrine

THE **Deification** SYNDROME

In two short years, he will be back. In the meantime, you and he have to decide how best to care for his treasures.

A dear friend of mine went through what I will refer to as the "deification syndrome." This is not an uncommon practice among moms of both girls and boys who either go on missions or go away to college. Some even stretch it to after the child is married, if room in the home permits. This can best be illustrated by a conversation I had with the daughter of a close friend. Of course, the names have been changed to preserve friendships.

"Lisa, now that Brian is gone, who has his room—you or Amy?"

"His room?" Lisa looked perplexed at the very thought. "My mother doesn't let anyone in his room! She's making it into a shrine, you know!"

When the children leave home, we are able to canonize them. The glaring faults they once possessed are never to be spoken of by family members. They are now saints in their own right, and the obvious tribute to the love we have for them is to leave their rooms intact. This monument symbolizes our devotion and is a sure sign that they will once again return, and things will be as they were.

Everything remains as it is: the clothes hanging in the closets; pictures on the walls; cologne, trinkets, books on the dresser; ticket stubs from concerts; and flowers from proms stuck in the corner of the mirror. All will remain exactly as it was left—right down to the dust bunnies under the bed!

This room becomes "the shrine." You can pass by the door of the shrine and longingly look in and picture your little boy or girl playing on the floor. You can go in and soak up the smells and ambiance and shed a few tears to assure yourself that you are, indeed, a loving mother. You can be sure that the other children in your family are giving appropriate homage to the missionary by guarding this shrine with your life and letting the other children know that any invasion of this space may result in penalties of great magnitude . . . or, *you can get a clue!*

The clue: Going on a mission is not something that we want our other children to view as sad. It's okay to let them know that mothers miss their children. That's a fact. However, you do not want them to think that a mission is something dismal and dreaded, and that's why mom is creating the shrine. Also, keep in mind that while this enshrining process may seem natural to you, it might be something your husband can neither understand nor agree with. In fact, he may think his previously strong and capable sweetheart is losing it!

There are actually pros and cons to preserving your missionary's space in the home. If you go overboard and lock the door to his bedroom, symbolically leaving the proverbial candle in the window, you may cause distress to siblings who have, heretofore, had access to this room. You also, thereby, set yourself up as the guardian or defender of the shrine.

Going from one extreme to the other, an elder who was serving in our ward shared his concern about the fact that his mother had immediately turned his room into a sewing room for herself. He spent at least a small portion of time during his mission wondering if, and how, he would be able to reclaim his personal space in the house.

After his return home, he called, and I asked if he had regained custody of his room. He had found that this was not as easy as he thought and that he still had some of his mom's stuff in the corner. Perhaps she thought he would be leaving for school or planning to move out when he returned, but, obviously, this was not the case. As a matter of fact, he sounded like they might be enjoying his company for a good long while!

This is, of course, an additional situation that is personal in nature and different for each family. Some parents have made it ever so lovingly known that when a child finishes high school, he is going somewhere! He may be going on a mission, going to college, going into the military, going to work and getting his own apartment—but he is definitely going! He will, in some situation, some place, be finding his own living accommodations and learning his own survival skills.

Other parents feel that to accomplish things deemed valuable, their child should remain home a little longer for financial, educational, or emotional reasons. Some families believe children should remain in the home until married, and this is very often a common thing in certain cultures.

With that being said, the point is that totally demolishing any resemblance of the missionary's old room may be a little hard for him to take. For two years, he imagines returning to the nest, a conquering hero, to the waiting arms of an adoring family. To make his return seem like an inconvenience in any way could be quite demoralizing.

So, how do you handle it? Family dynamics tend to set the path for what will be done with the precious space abandoned by your missionary. In many cases, a younger sibling is lurking in the wings, waiting to take over the rest of the space in a shared room or move into a new room. Of course, there are moms, as was mentioned, who envision a craft or sewing room and dads who see a study or home office. It would be wise to give this matter considerable thought; two years go by more quickly than you think, and soon you will again have decisions to make regarding the coveted space.

There are two things to consider, the room and the stuff. In most cases, the missionary will not have control over what happens to his room, but his personal items are another story. Here's a suggestion that tends to give peace of mind to everyone in the family. Make your departing missionary a partner in how things will be handled. The last thing your missionary needs to worry about is whether a little brother is destroying his favorite baseball glove or whether her personal journal is being taken to show-and-tell.

Acquire several large boxes and a roll of packing tape. Have your missionary clean out closets and drawers, packing away, giving away, and throwing away items as deemed appropriate. Let's face it, this has probably needed to be done for a long time anyway!

Actually, this can be fun. You can reminisce together as you pull out items that bring back memories of his childhood and decide what treasures should be kept forever. Perhaps a favorite football could get passed on to a younger brother, or a favorite sweater could go to a younger sister, allowing for a moment of love and bonding. It worked well for my sons to go through their closets and drawers, passing some things on to younger brothers and packing other things away.

All treasures, clothes, books, memorabilia, sporting equipment, and so forth were packed neatly in boxes, labeled, and closed with tape, insuring they would be safe until their owner's return. Some were stored in the room, others in the garage, but after two years, they were all lovingly and happily unpacked by their rightful owner.

This method accomplishes four things:

1. The missionary knows his wealth is protected. Things that really matter have been sorted out and placed in a safe place. He will not need to worry about them until he returns.

2. You have gone through a ritual that sets a standard for others who will leave. You have actually set a tradition for other missionaries and college students leaving home for the first time.

3. You have performed something cathartic in nature that will help you deal with the empty space in your nest.

4. You are now freed from the responsibility of being guardian of the stuff. You are no longer the ogre under the bridge, watching for those who are trying to storm the castle, or the evil mom who loves the absent son or daughter more than the ones left at home. You have eliminated one

unnecessary responsibility. Just watch out for younger children headed to the garage with a box cutter!

It doesn't help when the family dog patiently
waits by the window.

THE **Farewell** SACRAMENT MEETING TALK

In some cases, this can be the day your missionary has been dreading. Proper preparation and perspective will help to make it enjoyable and memorable.

I have yet to meet any parents or children who have said they looked forward to the "farewell" sacrament meeting. Okay, okay, we don't call them that anymore and, as of this time, the parents no longer speak in that meeting. However, the fact remains that, in most cases, there is a sacrament meeting before a young man leaves on his mission at which he and usually two others will speak. These other two speakers are sometimes requested by the missionary, or they may be suggested by the bishop. In general, the bishop will assign a subject on which they are to speak. This meeting is no longer meant to be a eulogy of sorts for the departing missionary.

This may be especially difficult for you as a mother because this is the last big event before this now-sinless, perfect-in-every-way, love-of-your-life child leaves for the longest two years ever recorded. Even for the stout of heart and those who don't mind speaking in public, it can be quite traumatic. This is probably one of the many reasons Church policy has changed to omit parents from speaking at this time.

For many, this is a relief and for others, it is something they looked forward to, and now they feel cheated. It has always been a sort of "rite-of-passage of parenthood" and part of our grieving process to have this last opportunity to express all those things we didn't take time to do in the last nineteen years.

In thinking about this, I realized that many wards have very few missionaries leave in a year, but others have young men leaving every month. What if all of our sacrament meetings took on the look of one I vividly recall?

Upon entering the chapel, I immediately knew it was a missionary farewell. The members of the family sat on the stand, stone-faced, not a smile among them. Now and again, the husband would pat his wife on the knee and give her "the look." It was the "Honey, we done good" look. She in turn would pat the missionary and give him the "mommy loves you" look, and he in turn would blankly stare at his shoes.

At the appropriate time, the mother got up to give her talk. Prior to this, I wouldn't have guessed that she had a single problem with her salivary glands. Now they completely failed her, and every word into the microphone brought forth a dry smacking sound. The much dreaded "cotton mouth" had set in. Perhaps her salivary glands had dried up in response to the heavy call for fluid by her tear ducts. There simply wasn't enough moisture to go around!

All in all, the mom was splendid. She managed to cover the subject the bishop had assigned while interjecting enough embarrassing material to give her son something to treasure for the rest of his life, including the day and time he was toilet trained. Alright, maybe she didn't talk about that, but it was just as embarrassing!

Now it was dad's turn. He was stalwart. He had been away on business for a week and hadn't had time to worry about his talk. As a matter of fact, he hadn't written his talk until he was on the plane coming home. This would account for the fact that his notes were written on the back of business cards and in the margin of the Skymall Magazine. Nonetheless, he nobly imparted pearls of wisdom to his son who, by the way, was still staring at his shoes.

In the waiting young man's mind, it seemed the most important thing about his parents' talks was that they were long enough to take up most of the time. Most missionaries don't have a lot to say when they leave on a mission, but they make up for it when they come home.

So, what can we do to help these up-and-coming defenders of the truth make it through this important speaking assignment? If, in fact, there is any indication that your help would be appreciated, here are a few suggestions:

- Encourage him to do as much research and preparation on his own as talent and time permits. You won't be there the first time he has to speak at zone conference! However, he will most likely appreciate being supplied with books and other resource material.
- Remind him to stick to the subject assigned while

including scriptures and interesting stories perti-
nent to the topic.

- The best talks are those that are *not* read, or at the
  very least, include stories that can be related from
  memory.

- If the speaker understands the material, he will
  more easily be able to deliver it from memory.
  He should not try to relate concepts that are over
  his head, but rather rely on basics or things that
  are at his particular level. If he doesn't understand
  the material, he will probably not deliver it to his
  audience in a pleasing or understandable manner.

- The fact is, as wonderful as your missionary's talk
  may turn out, he will probably not be asked to
  stay home from his mission and join the "Know
  Your Religion" circuit. When preparing, the missionary should ask himself if the time spent in the
  meeting will be enlightening and uplifting to
  those in the congregation. Will they leave feeling edified? Does his material cover the subject
  assigned by the bishop? Will the members hear
  his testimony and know of his love for the Savior
  and of the work he is about to do? Will they see
  that this young man has reached a point in his
  life where he is willing and prepared to serve the
  Lord?

This is the most that we can hope for. Some do better
than others. Be thrilled that your son or daughter is about
to be part of the Lord's work, to touch lives, and perhaps start someone on the path to exaltation. When he
gets home, you will probably be amazed at the spiritual
growth that has taken place, and you can be confident
that he won't ask for help with his talk upon his return!

"Elder Green, isn't this great? We have ten minutes left before curfew and only one more book to place to beat the zone record!"

Seeing Him Off

or But I'm Not Through

with Him Yet!

Whether at the airport, bus station, or Missionary Training Center, this last contact for two years is a difficult and highly emotional time for all.

We are fortunate to now have missionary training centers in many parts of the world; whereas the MTC in Provo used to be the only one. If your missionary is going to a country that has its own training center, more than likely, you will be saying good-bye at your local airport. Otherwise, you might be planning on dropping him off in Provo. This is, of course, a matter of choice.

Frankly, one place is no easier than the other to part with your child for two years. You know that this is the last moment you will see his face, hug him, and, yes, shed a few tears. In theory, if you are at your local airport, you have more last minutes to share. You must know, that at this time, if you accompany your child to Provo, you will pull your car up in front of the MTC, drop your missionary off, have a moment for a short hug and kiss and drive away. You will notice that I said one car and not a convoy of relatives and friends! It is encouraged that your car contain only a few immediate family members. I can attest to you, personally, that this is for the best.

Two of the more harrowing experiences of my life occurred while accompanying my friend, a single mother, as she saw her first son off at the Salt Lake Airport and then, several years later, as we dropped her "baby" off at the MTC under the old program.

As we met the oldest son at the airport, I immediately noticed that he was very composed and mostly concerned about his mother. She, on the other hand, was not at all composed. Instantly, upon seeing his face, she realized she was not through with him yet!

We had a little over an hour to chat, and she managed to tearfully babble for the entire time without regard as to whether she was making much sense or whether or not anyone else was overhearing. There seemed to be so much to tell and things that had not yet been taught that needed to be wedged into these last few moments. I figured it was my duty and obligation to take the focus away from her, so I began talking to the other waiting parents, thinking I was creating a diversion. Her son handled things remarkably well and placated her in all of her last-minute advice.

In retrospect, I'm sure she was trying to find the logic in telling a child not to talk to strangers for eighteen years and then sending him off to a foreign country and telling him to knock on doors, go into strange houses, and even strike up conversations with people on the streets!

Eventually, after what seemed like seconds to her, but hours to me, the flight attendant called for everyone to board the plane. My friend continued to hang onto her son, giving last-minute instructions. In time, the attendant was calling for the final, absolute-last, no-matter-what, if-you-don't-hurry-we'll-leave-you boarding call. Her son was trying to make his way down the ramp as she still clung to her last minutes of motherhood . . . and his sleeve. I could see that she needed my support, and I grasped her wrist tightly and pried her white knuckles from his arm.

Well, we made it through, and for the rest of the weekend we shopped, visited the genealogy library, and did girl stuff to forget our troubles.

Back to the MTC. Same friend—but this time it was the baby of the family that was leaving. For those of you who remember the old program, you will relate to this. And the rest of you will get a chuckle out of the story.

We were late getting to the MTC, and they hurried us into a presentation that was already in progress. We were able to hear the talks and most of the film, but obviously hadn't seen the whole thing. Nevertheless, the officiator soon said that it was time to say good-bye and that the missionaries would exit to the right and the parents to the left.

Through her tears and in her frantic attempt to grab a few more precious moments with her son, she became overwhelmed by the fact that we hadn't seen the whole presentation. There was no pacifying her. She wasn't about to exit anywhere until she sat through a complete presentation.

I took her son aside and asked if he realized how much his mother loved him and that it was making her a little crazy at the moment. He said he did but didn't know what to do. He stayed with her, and I found a pleasant lady in the hallway who pointed me to a room where another program was about to start. After that presentation, my friend knew she had run out of cards and that the game was over. After several more hugs and kisses, he was able to make his getaway and catch up with his group.

I know I'm telling this story with tongue in cheek, but that's actually the way it happened. This was a heart-wrenching experience for my friend, and I remembered those pains all too well. The only way I held back my own tears was realizing that it would only make her worse. She was fortunate that her sons very much understood their mother and also understood that this was just her love for them pouring out through her tear ducts.

If possible, try to control these feelings and put a "stiff upper lip" in their place to lift your missionary's spirits. Within minutes, he will be with his new family, the other young men with whom he will spend his training experience. He will want to muster up all of the strength and maturity he can to impress them. Within days, most parents receive letters that make them wonder why they ever worried about their missionary or wasted tears in his behalf. This is a marvelous, once-in-a-lifetime experience and every missionary I've talked to loved the time he spent at the MTC.

This whole story is designed to let you know that the day you drop your son off at the airport, you may suddenly remember all those very important things that you didn't tell him or teach him. This adds to your emotional distress and can thwart your efforts in remaining calm and positive.

When seeing one of my sons off at the Salt Lake

Airport, I was really having a hard time choking back the tears, and I could tell it was affecting him. There was a lot going on, and I tried to concentrate on anything other than how much time we had left. My son's MTC companion was from Idaho, and his whole family was there to see him off, complete with cowboy hats and enormous silver belt buckles. His mom had brought his favorite blueberry cheesecake and was handing it out to any who cared to indulge. This was definitely a mom who was in control of her feelings!

I was upset enough that I couldn't even eat cheesecake! I did my best to gain control and did fairly well. However, there was another mom with whom I could empathize who had totally broken down. She was sobbing uncontrollably, and in a short time her son was doing the same.

I didn't worry as much about her as I did about him. I knew he was boarding the plane feeling sad and embarrassed, though none of the other missionaries appeared to be thinking any the worse of him. I imagined, and I think rightfully so, that the young man in question was able to contain himself relatively soon and did just fine. However, do consider that some of our young men return home simply because they are so homesick that they cannot concentrate on their work. We must do our best to keep our feelings in check so as to not add to this situation.

If you and your family have been preparing for this day, physically and spiritually, for his whole life, you are a step ahead of the rest. You have done everything you can and now you have but one task, to call on the Spirit of the Lord in his behalf and your own.

Return WITH **Honor**

Two years have gone by, and he's home. What does he expect? What can you expect? Will things ever be the same?

He's back! The scene at the airport was all that you wanted it to be. Friends and family, balloons and banners, hugs, laughter, and tears of joy.

The first few days he followed you around the house. It would seem that being in the constant presence of a companion had grown to be a habit! In fact, you had to remind him that there were times that you appreciated your privacy. Suddenly, he loved doing things with the family or even going grocery shopping with mom. This was great! You always wanted such a devoted son.

At first, he was not comfortable watching television or listening to the radio unless it was the Disney Channel or Church tapes. His girlfriend had written him a "Dear John," but that was okay because the perfect girl for him had moved into the ward, and you had only to introduce them. He had decided, while in the mission field, that he would continue getting up at 5 AM to study the scriptures and make that a lifelong habit. He was on his knees morning and night. How could you ask for more? He had returned with honor. He loved the members, contacts, and companions he had left behind and couldn't wait to take you on a trip to visit.

Strangely, two weeks to a month later, things seemed to be changing. The alarm went off at five, but only to be slammed off with a thud, waking everyone in the house but its owner. Friends were assisting in bringing him up to date with suitable clothing, music, and videos that he had missed. An entire week went by without his razor coming anywhere near his face. This returned missionary became a new and ambitious member of the young adult ward, and there was no lack of young women to make him feel welcome.

So, in answer to the question, "Will things ever be the same," the answer is NO. As a matter of fact, you probably won't be sure how they are going to be for some time. There are so many variables.

Is he planning on going to college? Does he need to work before that can be accomplished? Does he have a strong desire to marry right away, or are there other things he wants to do first? Is there still a place for him at home, or will he need to make plans to be on his own? All of the answers depend, in part, on family policy set up before he left.

So what do we know? We know that while your son was on his mission, the Spirit of the Holy Ghost gave him a sort of super momentum. It was as if a hand was physically on his back pushing him along, making his steps lighter and his hardships more bearable.

I once heard a missionary compare it to being on a people mover at the airport. You are walking, but a power is moving you faster and with less effort, and you reach your destination or goal with powers that are not your own. This missionary also said that coming home from your mission is like the end of the people mover. Your feet come to the end of this fast moving track and, suddenly, all the weight is on your shoulders, and every step becomes more difficult.

Bishops and stake presidents describe a similar occurrence when they are released from their callings. When the mantel of a calling is removed, things such as the power of discernment or revelation in behalf of a specific group may be gone. This is not a bad thing; it's just part of the plan. God assists us in duties to which we are called.

I believe the most powerful statement I have heard uttered by a returned missionary is that, while on his mission, he learned to *recognize* the voice of the Lord. I have to emphasize that because it is such a profound blessing. Though the returned missionary may go through this feeling of not having the Holy Ghost directing his every move, he will soon realize that it is probably because he is not listening as intently. With his constant prayer and obedience to the commandments, the Holy Ghost will still be his constant companion and guide and direct him in his new course, with his new goals and callings. He is not giving anything up, just climbing new steps toward exaltation. He will even find a new study schedule—but maybe not at 5 AM.

As parents, we are now in a position of "shadow leadership." We are dealing with an adult who has had to obey the rules of the mission and should still obey the rules of your household, but who has been responsible for himself for two years. He is now twenty-one years old. That, in itself, gives him a feeling of rights and power to decide for himself. In some cases, we are delighted at the maturity level he has achieved and how capable he is of making great decisions. Probably, in more cases, we become aware that, though he has matured in many areas, he still has a lot of growing up to do. You will handle this part of parenting just as you did his early years.

Right now, you can revel in the fact that your son has served an honorable mission. He touched lives and planted seeds and may have baptized people. Or perhaps your son did not baptize anyone. This can be very difficult to deal with, and he may feel like a failure or like he wasted two years.

There is absolutely no way that this is possible. First, we know that he was and will continue to be blessed for his sacrifice. Second, we know that there are areas in the world where the gospel is being taught, but conversions are few at any given time. Third, we never know what may occur when we plant a seed. It may bear fruit long after we are gone and may be more prolific than we could have imagined.

I am such an example of planting a seed. The missionaries who first taught me the gospel have no idea that I was ever baptized. They have no idea that I have been through the temple, have worked diligently in the Church for thirty-five years, and have sent three missionaries of my own into the field.

Your family structure is changing, but in another sense it is eternal. You are doing well. Seeing children through a mission is, in fact, part of *your* mission on this earth. You have accomplished that which has been asked of you. You are one step closer to that glorious day when you will be reunited with your eternal family and hear the words, "Well done, thou good and faithful servant" (Matthew 25:21).

Acknowledgments

There are too many names to acknowledge all who have helped me in writing this book. This is true in all things, as all that have touched our lives for good have added strength to our convictions and given us the fuel and inspiration necessary to carry out and accomplish our goals.

My mother, Madeline Goyeneche, always believed that I could accomplish anything that I desired. Her love and support have extended to my children and grandchildren, and her greatest desire seems to be to provide the "wind beneath our wings." Though she is not a member of the LDS Church, and though the years have taken her eyesight, she has championed and taken pride in the publication of this work. She is my head cheerleader.

My husband, Mel, is my best critic—best in that he loves everything I do, or at least he makes me think so! It has been so wonderful having a companion who I know will always have something good to say. I must also acknowledge his magnificent missionary zeal and the effort he has given to growing the Church throughout his life.

To my sons, thank you for letting me practice my mothering skills and for not complaining when I didn't get it right. I'm also grateful for the fodder you have provided for this book and for your continued love and support. Know that I will love you always.

Thanks to my dear friend Dr. Kevin Theriot for reviewing this work and adding the wonderful foreword. He has been a special strength in my life for many years.

My friend from Health Plus Publishers, Karen Lyman, deserves my deepest thanks for listening to every chapter (no matter what the hour) and giving her honest opinion. She is also one of the anonymous mothers mentioned in this book who supplied material with her experiences and love for her missionary sons.

Corey Smith took pity on me for my lack of computer skills and spent hours helping me prepare my manuscript for submission. Thanks to him and his son, John, for their kindness and time away from their business to aide a friend.

Also, my appreciation to Paul Howalt of Tactix Creative for "polishing up" my artwork and to my editor, Heidi Doxey, and the others at Cedar Fort, Inc., who helped to prepare this work for publication.

Last but not least, thanks to Jerri Jones and Michelle LeCheminant, stalwart friends and missionary mothers, who gave me encouragement, listened to each word written and spurred me on.